TOP SPEEDS

HORSE — 75 KM (46 MILES) PER HOUR

ELECTRIC SKATEBOARD — 37 KM (23 MILES) PER HOUR

DOG — 70 KM (43.5 MILES) PER HOUR

JET PLANE —3,530 KM (2,193 MILES) PER HOUR   NOW THAT'S FAST!: AIRCRAFT

RABBIT — 72 KM (45 MILES) PER HOUR

HUMAN — 45 KM (28 MILES) PER HOUR

BIKE — 132 KM (82 MILES) PER HOUR

NOW THAT'S FAST!
AIRCRAFT

KATE RIGGS

FRANKLIN WATTS
LONDON • SYDNEY

First published in the UK in 2011 by
Franklin Watts
338 Euston Road
London NW1 3BH

Franklin Watts Australia
Level 17/207 Kent Street
Sydney NSW 2000

First published by Creative Education,
an imprint of the Creative Company.
Copyright © 2010 Creative Education
International copyright reserved in all countries.
No part of this book may be reproduced in any
form without written permission from
the publisher.

ISBN 978 1 4451 0584 0
Dewey number: 629.1'3334

A CIP catalogue record for this book
is available from the British Library.

Printed in China

Franklin Watts is a division of
Hachette Children's Books,
an Hachette UK company.
www.hachette.co.uk

Book and cover design by Blue Design
(www.bluedes.com)
Art direction by Rita Marshall

Photographs by Corbis (Patrick Bennett, Bettmann),
Dreamstime (Gvision, Sportslibrary), Getty
Images (PATRICK HERTZOG/AFP, Simeone Huber,
FRANCISCO LEONG/AFP, JEFF PACHOUD/AFP,
Piotr Powietrzynski, Quinn Rooney, Martin Rose/
Bongarts, Topical Press Agency), iStockphoto
(Arthur Achtelik)
Every atttempt has been made to clear copyright.
Should there be any inadvertent omission, please
contact the publisher for rectification.

A jet is a high-powered aircraft. Jets have powerful **engines** which means that they can fly higher and faster than other planes. Most jets that carry a lot of people go at about 933 km (580 miles) per hour. Smaller jets can travel at more than 2,092 km (1,300 miles) per hour!

Skilled workers called engineers look after jet engines.

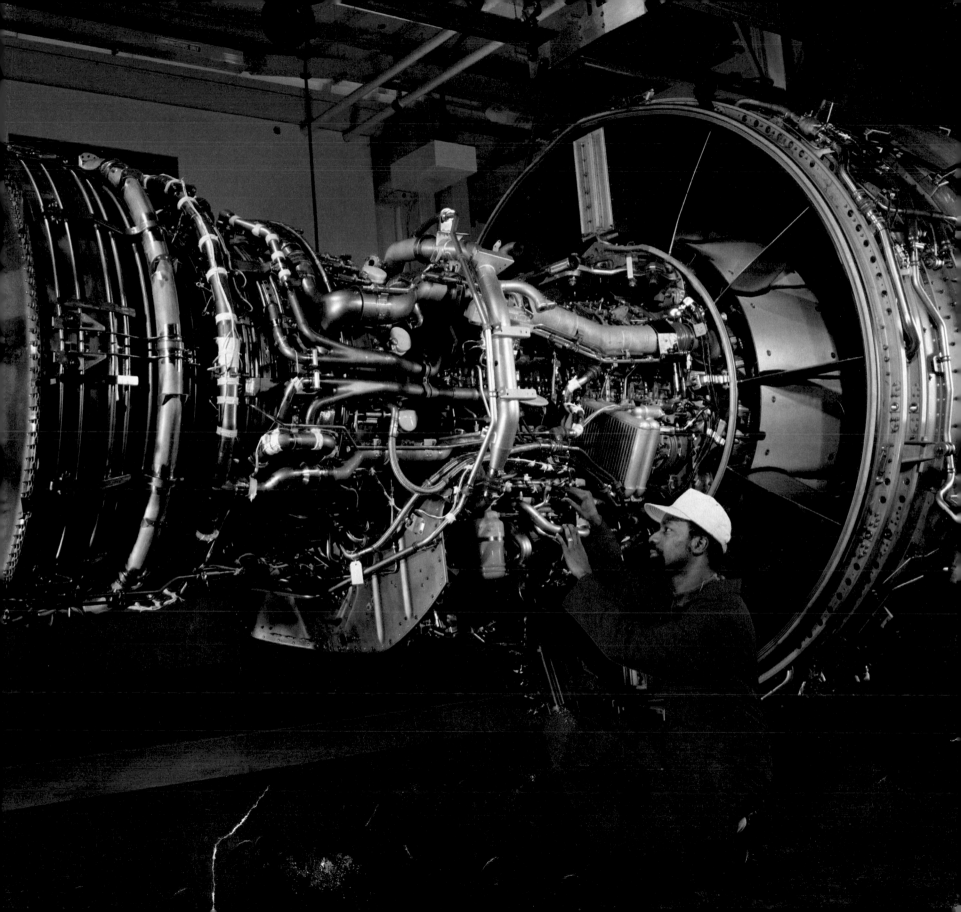

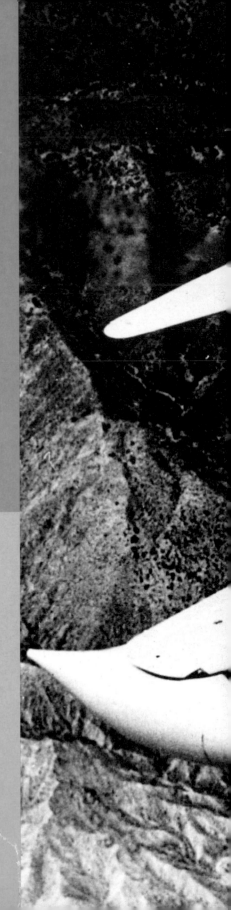

The first jet engines were made in the 1930s. Some of the first jets were built in Great Britain. They were used by the army as fighter planes. These jets had guns on them.

Fighter planes often have nicknames, such as this 'Shooting Star', built in the USA.

All jet planes have a main part called the body. The wings are attached to it. The front of the jet is called the nose.

Most **commercial** jets have wide bodies. Other jets have narrow bodies.

A jet's engines are attached to its wings.

Engine

When a jet is ready to land,
it puts down its wheels.

Jets are used for different purposes. Most commercial jets are used to carry passengers around the world, usually for work or to go on holiday.

An Airbus A380 jet has four
powerful engines.

The biggest aircraft are called jumbo jets. The first jumbo, the Boeing 747, was   in the 1970s. It could carry over 500 passengers and fly thousands of kilometres non-stop. Today, the Airbus A380 can transport over 800 passengers at a time.

People can also fly in private aircraft. Small planes only carry a few people at a time so they are a very expensive way to fly! They are usually only used to make short journeys.

Private aircraft are used to travel quickly and comfortably from place to place.

Jets can fly very high up in the air. At first, jets could only fly up to 3,000 m (9,842 feet) above the ground. But now jets fly at about 12,000 m (39,370 feet). The air is thinner there, which makes the ride smoother.

Jets fly high up in the sky to avoid clouds and bad weather.

Fighter aircraft are designed to fight other planes. They are very small, light and fast. They can travel at amazing speeds of over 3,000 kph and make quick, tight twists and turns to help them escape enemy planes.

Fighter jets sometimes fly together in a group called a formation.

The pilot controls the aircraft. He or she sits in the **cockpit** and keeps in touch with **air traffic controllers** on the ground during the flight to make sure that the flight is safe and smooth. The pilot is always ready to take another ride through the skies!

Fast Facts

The first manned jet flight took place in Germany in 1939.

An English man named Frank Whittle was one of the first jet engine inventors.

Wide-bodied jets such as jumbo jets can carry between 200 and 600 passengers.

The Lockheed SR-71 Blackbird is one of the fastest jets ever. It has flown at more than 3,500 km per hour!

Glossary

air traffic controllers – people who guide planes safely through the skies

cockpit – the place where the pilot sits in a plane

commercial – something that is used to make money

engines – machines inside vehicles that make them move

invent – to come up with the idea of how to make a new thing

passengers – people who travel on a jet or other vehicle

private aircraft – a plane or helicopter that is owned or hired by a person or a company to make a journey

Read More about It

Extreme Machines: Planes
David Jefferis, Franklin Watts 2009

Web Site

Boeing Kids Page
http://www.boeing.com/companyoffices/aboutus/kids/coloring.html
This site has pictures of jets that can be coloured in.

Index

air traffic controllers 22
cockpit 22
commercial jets. 10, 13
engines 6, 8, 10, 14, 23
fighter jets 8, 21, 23
Great Britain 8
jet bodies 10
jumbo jets 15, 23
passengers 13, 15, 23
pilots. 22
private aircraft 16
speeds. 1, 6, 21, 23